IRELAND FOR BEGINNERS

or

Get Lost in Ireland

Rupert Besley

'May the road rise up to meet you...'

While every reasonable care has been taken in compiling this book, the author and publisher regret they cannot be held responsible for any accuracy or correct details that may occur in the text.

BARNES
&NOBLE
BOOKS
NEW YORK

© Rupert Besley, 1994

This edition published by
Barnes & Noble Inc., by
arrangement with
Neil Wilson Publishing Ltd.
1996 Barnes & Noble Books.

The moral right of the author has been asserted.

ISBN-0-7607-0052-4

Typeset in 9/10pt Bodoni by Face to Face Design Services, Glasgow.

Printed in UAE by Oriental Press.

M 10 9 8 7 6 5 4 3 2

Contents

Arrival

A faint blur in the greyness, the hint of a shape through the mist ... that first glimpse of Ireland is a magical moment, which visitors stop to savour as they make their way down the ship's gangway or aircraft steps. No matter which way you choose to arrive (sea and air are the most popular ways), you'll have a sense of joy and thanksgiving as you take your first wobbly steps on dryish land.

Look around and see if you can count the famous forty shades of green!

40 SHADES OF GREEN

THE SEARCH FOR ROOTS

Do not be surprised to find your fellow-travellers sinking to their knees and kissing the tarmac — crossing the Irish Sea often has that effect on people.

Whether you come by car or land as a foot-passenger, make the most of your arrival, pausing perhaps to enjoy the little rituals of passport, customs and that amusing spray of disinfectant which signals your entry into IRELAND OF THE WELCOMES.

As they say in Ireland, Céad Míle Fáilte!

Or translated, Here Comes Another One.

THE IRISH SEA

Geography
Location & Topography

WHERE IS IT?

Ireland is the large area generally hidden by the weatherman when the British Isles appear on your screen. Northern Ireland is sometimes glimpsed beneath the forecaster's armpit when deepening depressions in Shetland and the Faroes call for a cheery wave around the top of the map.

Neatly poised midway between America and whatever Russia calls itself nowadays, Ireland is well-placed to occupy a central position in the modern world. For those hopping over the Atlantic, Ireland is the doormat to Europe. For those going west, Ireland is the last point of civilisation for many thousands of miles.

Though relations may have seemed at times distant and even frosty, Ireland has always sought in foreign affairs to keep up a close and cordial relationship with her nearest neighbours on each side — Britain and the United States to east and west, South Georgia and the North Pole in the other directions.

WHAT'S IT LIKE?

First-time visitors to Ireland are often disconcerted to find that the country does not consist entirely of bog. 'Where's the bog?' they cry at every stop on the coach tour. Bogs cover only one-seventh of the country, parts of which — like The Burren — are notably un-squelchy.

Ireland is well and truly spattered with lakes. Ireland also has plenty of rivers, most of which usually turn out to be the Shannon. This mighty river sets off on its 214-mile journey from a small pot in Co. Cavan.

Mountains in Ireland tend to stick around the edge of the country. Most bear the Irish name for mountain, which is Slieve. Hill-walkers can enjoy long-slieve and short-slieve routes, as well as parts which are entirely slieve-less. Northern Ireland is mostly hilly, except for the Lakes of Fermanagh, which are surprisingly flat.

Generally likened to a saucer in shape, Ireland is flat in the centre and raised at the edge, with an awful lot of water slopping about in the middle. Perhaps a better comparison would be with a lettuce-leaf: green and crumpled, frayed at the edges and ninety per cent water. Not forgetting the odd nasty clinging to its underside or lurking in the folds.

The boglands are rich in wildlife

Bog bean

Bog cotton

Bog brush

7

DIVISIONS

As everyone knows, Ireland is divided.

In the first place there is the division between north and south. Thus, South Down is up in Northern Ireland, whereas North Ring is right down in the South. Malin Head, the northernmost point of Ireland, is in Southern Ireland. The border between North and South (also known as Ulster and Eire, The Province and The Republic or simply Them and Us) is 303 miles long on its northern side and 280 along the south.

After the north-south divide comes the division into provinces and counties. Ulster, for example, has nine counties — three in the Republic and six in the North. The seventh usually turns out to be Lough Neagh.

8

ISLANDS

Set like a precious jewel in a cluster of smaller gems, the Great Emerald of Ireland is encircled by a multitude of lesser isles, from Great Blasket in the west to Great Britain in the east. The Irish coastline is littered with skerries and countless small islands, 365 in all.

Most famous of these are the Arans, thanks to the film *Man of Aran* shown to all visitors three times a day. Patiently constructed by generations of hardy islanders from alternating layers of sand and seaweed, the Aran Islands face the constant onslaught of pounding seas and perilous visitors.

Many of Ireland's islands are no longer inhabitable. Such are the Skelligs, off Kerry, once home to monks who lived in beehives. Likewise the Blaskets, which include at Ireland's westernmost point the small island of Inishvickillane, to which in recent years the Irish Prime Minister was regularly banished by the people of Dublin, when they felt they could take no more.

Caution: Do not confuse Clare Island (not near Clare) with Clear Island (not there either) or Aran Island (also known as Aranmore or Arranmore, but not Arran, which is in Scotland) with the Aran Islands, also off Ireland. These are called Inishmore, Inishmaan and Inisheer (or Inishere) — not to be confused with Inishbofin (either of them), Inishturk, Inishark, Inishkea (N or S) or even Inishmurray. Not to mention Inishbiggle.

Inishturk

Inishark

9

PEAT BOGS

Much of Ireland's central bogland is infertile, defying all bids at agriculture. Instead the peat is dug out and sold to English garden centres as an essential growing medium.

Elsewhere, in the blanket bogs of Ireland's periphery, peat is still extracted to satisfy the energy needs of a growing population. All over Ireland, throughout the year, turf fires fitfully smoulder, filling the valleys with their sweet aroma. The unique property of turf is that it does give smoke without fire.

Peat-fired power-stations have long been a reality in Ireland, though hopes of finding more imaginative applications for Ireland's black gold (turf-powered cars, for example, or peat-burning pocket calculators) have so far come to nought.

Prototype Ford O'Ryan

Peat drying

Cutting turf is basically a simple process. Take flachter to scraw, then cut by slane, removing turves by trundle, slide-car or slipe. Cutters work in steady rhythm, picking their way cautiously round the many remains of Iron Age bodies concealed in the peat. Ireland today has many Folk Museums and Rural Life Exhibitions which enable the visitor to study at leisure exhaustive displays of old spades.

Following centuries of tradition, the cut turves are put into plastic bags and then set out in optimistic piles by the roadside to dry. Here they are periodically checked and counted by the proper authorities (you will no doubt have seen the busy offices of Turf Accountants in most small Irish towns) and then removed by tourists.

Climate

Ireland enjoys an equable climate, which means there's not much difference between the seasons. Or, as cynics put it, summer's when the rain warms up a bit. The Ancients, who knew a thing or two, reckoned on only two seasons in Ireland: summer (which began — and often ended — on May Day) and winter (the rest of the time). The Romans, looking out for new places to invade in their summer hols, named it Winter (Hibernia) and stayed away. All of which is most unfair on the Irish climate, which is varied and fast-moving. Weather-systems track in at great speed from the Atlantic, leaving ever decreasing gaps between showers.

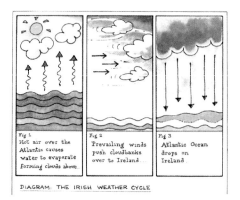

DIAGRAM. THE IRISH WEATHER CYCLE

Fig 1 Hot air over the Atlantic causes water to evaporate forming clouds above.

Fig 2 Prevailing winds push cloudbanks over to Ireland.

Fig 3 Atlantic Ocean drops on Ireland.

RAIN

The Irish generally deny the existence of rain, but they do own up to the occasional 'soft day' or 'touch of mist'. This mist comes bucketing down most days. Only the eastern edge of Ireland gets away with less than 200 rainy days per annum.

Rainfall is heaviest in the west and over high ground (see diagram). The raised bogs of Mayo, for example, annually receive more than 50in of rain, which is bad news for anyone 4ft tall or under. 141in of water fell on the Ring of Kerry in 1903. Belfast, by contrast, is regularly under 35in of rainfall.

Over the years the soft weather has enabled the Irish to show much ingenuity in devising new ways of keeping dry. The ulster is an Irish invention. Likewise the submarine and the wellington boot, the latter dreamt up by the Iron Duke to wear out riding on his rusty steed.

Three-man umbrellas are traditional
along the West Coast of Ireland.

WIND

Besides rain, a good deal of Ireland suffers from wind. Again, the west coast is the worst affected, with stiff Atlantic breezes regularly lifting the lid on the bogs of Munster. In Donegal, thatched rooves are traditionally held down by the 'hairnet-and-hatpin' system, with varying degrees

of success. Wind strength and direction can always be checked by visiting Glencar in Sligo to see which way the waterfall is going.

THE HOT SOUTH

It's not all wind and rain in Ireland. Down in the south-west corner where the Gulf Stream comes ashore, the land is a blaze of warmth. Here flourish exotic species, lush palms and luxuriant tropical ferns. Strawberries grow into trees, whilst in the plantations, high on the rugged mountain-slopes, Irish Coffee beans bake in the westering sun.

ADVICE TO VISITORS

Wear sensible shoes (galoshes or flippers). Take precautions at all times. No self-respecting Irishman would dream of ever leaving the house without first slipping a small packet into his trouser-pocket. This contains a plastic raincoat.

Looks like it's clouding over again —

Natural history

Ireland has a distinctive but limited range of flora and fauna. This is mainly due to Ireland having become a separate island long before Britain (Brits kindly note: Ireland got there first). When the last glaciers melted and seas rose, wiping out the land-bridge, only certain species were able to hop aboard before Ireland finally broke away and sailed off into the sunset. Half of them — plants especially — failed to jump the gap. Aquatic vegetation did rather better, managing to wade across.

So it is that Ireland misses out on all sorts of creatures — wild cats and woodpeckers, harvest-mice and nightingales, warthogs and wildebeest. There's just one frog in Ireland and the place is devoid of weasels — apart from

Just one frog...

'Recent introductions...'

the Irish stoat, which is called a weasel. No voles (except for recent introductions) and no moles either, which could be said to lend Irish lawns a certain air of drab uniformity.

Thanks to St Patrick, there are no snakes in Ireland. Apart from the occasional grass-snake.

15

DOMESTIC ANIMALS

Ireland has at least seven dog-breeds all its own. These include the giant Irish wolfhound (or Hound of Ulster), the Irish water spaniel, the Irish setter, the Irish terrier and the Kerry Blue (frequently mistaken for a cheese). Still encountered in outlying rural parts is the Irish Bandog, a traditional breed of man-eating mastiff famous for its jaws of flame.

IRISH DOG·BREEDS

Irish Water Spaniel

Springer

Irish Upsetter

Kerry Blue

Giant Irish Wolfhound

The furtive drumlin ..

The Burren is famous for its cracks and fissures inhabited by unusual botanists. Cork and Kerry are home to creatures like the spotted slug, usually found in Spain and Portugal.

The boglands abound in wildlife, with a gratifyingly healthy population of midges.

In winter months the Irish coastline is packed out with visiting birdlife, leaving standing room only in some parts. Tired geese on long-haul flights swoop down on the slobs of Wexford. Here gather Bewick's swans and half the world's population of the rare Greenland white-fronted goose — a magnificent sight, except under snow.

History

History is still going on in Ireland and is therefore best avoided by all who know what's good for them. Ignore this and you soon discover that Irish history consists mainly of miseries and woes inflicted upon the residents by previous visitors.

In among the grim succession of invasions, massacre and famine the Irish did manage three brief periods of relative happiness, known as Golden Ages.

FIRST GOLDEN AGE

Ireland's earliest known residents were The Giant Elk and some mammoth reindeer. When they moved out, in came the builders of the megaliths. Overnight the country was transformed — holes dug, paths blocked, slabs erected and the whole place turned into a building-site. Bronze Age folk were obsessive Home Improvers, constantly shoving up new ancient monuments, many of which clearly never got finished. Not so Newgrange, built to catch the brief rays of the sun, which came out for just a few minutes on only one day of the year. This was The Dawn of History.

Meanwhile, in the shelter of their sturdy homes, the Builders started to twiddle around with bits of metal. They fashioned rings and circlets, gorgets and bracelets, torcs, more torcs and even torcs about torcs. Business was good, dolmens were selling and the bottom had yet to fall out of the lower end of the cheap jewellery trade. Truly this was a Golden Age.

Possible origins of the Bronze Age Burial Mound ...

SECOND GOLDEN AGE

Next came the Celts, who also had a Golden Age. This lasted for ages. The Celts were a hardy race, who didn't mind the weather. People at this time dressed mainly in brooches, belts and interesting gold ornaments.

However, old habits die hard and soon the Celts found themselves drawn irresistibly into the business of sticking up stones. Many of these stones bear inscriptions in Ogham, a form of early bar-coding which, then as now, no one could read.

In time the Celts moved on to more complicated structures, including different types of fortification: lisses, raths, cashews, cahirs and even cattle-forts, manned by cows. This was a society in which cattle played an important part, carrying out military exploits (The Cattle Raid of Cooley) and writing unreadable memoirs (The Book of the Dun Cow).

TARA

Celtic life centres on the Hill of Tara, a grassy mound with a lot of small kings sitting on it. Right at the top, on a

It says Now-Please-Wash-Your-Hands -

CATTLE·FORTS

hard seat, sat the Ard-Ri ('High King' or 'King of the Castle'), kept entertained through the long days by his minstrel bards. It was a tough job and seldom comfortable.

The post of 'file' (poet-storyteller) was, by contrast, something of a cushy number. His job it was to tell bedtime stories to the warrior-chiefs, as they sank in the hay, draining the last dregs of mead from their cow horns. The 'filí' (whose many descendants are still with us) soon developed the art of spinning out stories into endless cycles which were unstoppable. Rediscovered in the Celtic Revival of the last century, the tales of Deirdre and Maeve, Dermot and Grania still enjoy enormous popularity ('dermotitis') and are no doubt responsible for the Tara boom today.

MISTS AND LEGENDS

For most of its ancient past, Ireland was steeped in mists and legends. These persisted until the sun came up on the Dawn of History, thus ending the Dark Ages. This was followed by the onset of north-easterly Gaels.

Mists and legends pose a problem for modern historians trying to separate fact from fiction. There is plenty of evidence — geological and archaeological — to prove the existence of the giant Fionn mac Cumhail (pronounced Finn MacCool as a general rumhail). The same goes for Diarmuid and Gráinne (Dermot and Grania), Ireland's tragic star-crossed lovers, who may have given Romeo and Juliet an idea or two. Tír nan Óg (The Land of Youth) was a magical place to the west of Ireland, where the flowers always bloomed and the women never aged: nowadays we call it California. The deeds of legendary heroes (like the men of the Fianna, Big Jack Charlton and The Mighty Cuchumber) are recorded in tales from the Ulster, Fenian and Raleigh Cycles, all of which have stood the test of time. However, question-marks still hang over the Children of Lir, who were changed into swans for 900 years. Let alone Niall of the Nine Noses.

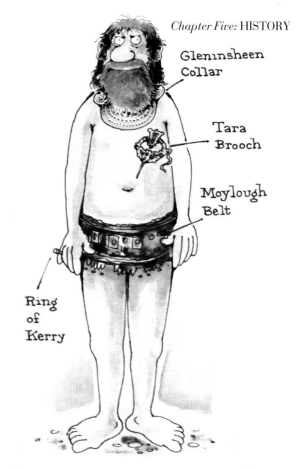

Gleninsheen Collar

Tara Brooch

Moylough Belt

Ring of Kerry

WHAT THE WELL-DRESSED CELT WORE

SAINTS AND SCHOLARS

To settle these squabbles, Ireland embarked upon a series of changes, which altered the course of its history. Things got written down in books and Christianity was introduced. So began the Era of Saints and Scholars.

At first there were only a few books — in fact, just the one book at Kells — which led to several nasty battles among the saints. Eventually the saints decided to paddle off to better places. The world was overrun with adventurous monks. Columba got to Iona, Brendan chose Florida and plucky St Gall crossed the Alps in his coracle to bring the good news to the Swiss.

With so many people out of the country, Ireland soon succumbed to attacks of the Vikings, sweeping down from the North. So ended Ireland's Second Golden Age.

VIKINGS, NORMANS AND OTHER VISITORS

Rudely interrupting the course of Irish History, the Vikings brought with them a number of nasty personal habits, like rapine, pillage and the eating of runes.

So unpleasant were the newcomers that the native population took to building tall towers in which to conceal themselves at the first sign of an approaching norseman. Grabbing their valuables, the local residents could stay hidden in their tower, undetected by the offensive marauder, until all danger passed. Even by Dark Age standards, Vikings must have been fairly dim.

The Vikings were finally wiped out by Brian Boru at Clontarf in the suburbs of Dublin. Next off the boat came the Normans, who were not much better. There followed several centuries of gloom and despondency, broken only by the building of Bunratty and Knappogue Castles in the fifteenth century, close to Shannon Airport. Both castles still ring to the sounds of non-stop jollity and feasting that have gone on there ever since.

THIRD GOLDEN AGE

Ireland meanwhile rumbled on with internal dissensions, not helped by the appearance of The Pail. Then came the Planters. Things changed only with the outbreak of the 18th century, a Golden Age in Ireland, unless you were Catholic or Irish.

This was the time of the Ascendancy, when Dublin's streets and squares were opened up and houses given doorways. The Ascendancy came to an abrupt end in the reign of George the Third (or George the Turd, as he is known in Irish) with a nasty attack of the troubles. Thereafter, Irish history distinctly took a down-turn, with famine, destitution and civil war, each too awful to dwell on.

THE IRISH PROBLEM

In 1160 the hopeless Dermot of Leinster sought help from the English in tackling a little local difficulty, which, 830-odd years on, is still no nearer a solution. This is what

PLANTERS

BORDER COUNTRY

is known as The Irish Problem, believed abroad to be rooted in the innate obstinacy and contrariness of the Irish people, with their longstanding refusal to accept absorption into a foreign power. Ireland joined the European Community in 1973.

Northern Ireland continues to face up to certain local difficulties. These are known as The Trobbles.

25

THE IRISH ABROAD

Famine forced millions of Irish to leave or die. Those who left, in search of work abroad, took on the dirty and unpleasant jobs that no one else would do — canal-digger, road-mender, American president ... Many found fame and fortune in far-flung places (Ned Kelly, Scarlett O'Hara, George Best). Others didn't.

Emigration has spread Irish folk across the globe, but also left the homeland distinctly short-staffed. Contrary to all the wisecracks, Ireland has

'Good news and bad, Mr O'Cromwell -'

the least dense population of Europe. Also the youngest. A large proportion of Ireland's population are — or have been — children. Large families are something of a necessity in Ireland, to fill in the gaps left by centuries of emigration.

TRACING YOUR ROOTS

Many of the Irish abroad are keen to establish their ancestry and Root-Tracing is big business now in Ireland. Each summer the countryside fills with friendly foreigners knocking on doors and trying to find our where they've come from.

26

Economy

Natural resources: water, peat
Principal export: nuns
Other exports: water, peat

The Industrial Revolution turned Belfast into a mighty manufacturing base (napkins and ocean liners), but otherwise passed most of Ireland by. The Irish Midlands are strangely free of belching chimneys and factory smoke.

Agriculture still plays an important part in the Irish

Cottage Industry

economy, from the shamrock-fields of the south to the wet uplands given over to the raising of Irish stew.

Olde worlde crafts are still plied in small cottages with sheep at the front, a loom at the back and the poteen frothing under the bed. Traditional products, such as cashmeres, Irish Dresden or the famous Belleek china (with its unusual open basket-weave design) make delightful souvenirs from local retailers. Shopping in Ireland is full of surprises.

Also much sought after by visitors is drink in any form. Whiskey goes down well at home and abroad, while continentals are invariably fascinated by the rich brown liqueur called Irish Mist. 'Mist' is the German for dung.

Currency note: the English pound (or 'punt' in Irish) no longer has parity with the Irish punt or pound. One is slightly more (or less) than the other and no-one can ever remember which.

Packet-switched satellite calls, enabling high-speed intercontinental data transmission, are now a regular feature of the Republic's digitalised microwave network and fibre-optic cables

Politics

Ever since Lloyd George first suggested putting up a partition across the country, the two Irelands have gone separate ways in political administration. Northern Ireland has tried most forms of government and is at present run by a secretary who flies to and fro. At ground-level, politicians come thick and fast. Most represent groupings which share a limited range of initials (DUP, UUP, OUP, SOUP, RUC, RAC, UVF, VHF, UDA, BUPA, SDLP, NILP etc). In terms of political alignment, true blues tend to be orange (or red, white and blue) and greens red.

Severing its last links with Britain in 1949, the Republic has developed its own system of government, headed by the Teashop. MPs are called TDs and meet in the Dáil. There are three main political parties: Fianna Fáil ('sol-diers of destiny'), Fine Gael ('wee Gaels') and the Irish Labour Party, usually known as 'Dick Spring'.

CAUTION

In Ulster, care should be taken not to confuse Republicans (who parade in the streets with flags and drums) with Loyalists (who parade in the streets with flags and drums).

National feelings run high on both sides of the border. For most Irish people in the south and elsewhere in the world, celebrations are focused upon March 17th, St Patrick's Day — a chance to drown the shamrock and honour the memory of the Bristol-born saint. Loyalists in the north meanwhile concentrate their attentions upon July 12th, anniversary of the Dutch King William of Orange's victory by the Boyne over troops who were mostly French. This took place on what was then July 1st, 1690.

National fervour on this scale is something indigenous to the Celtic soul, but rarely understood by the unromantic British. The Celts came from India.

In Northern Ireland political loyalties are of course a matter of personal discretion and private concern ...

Religion

Ireland has lots of religion. Indeed, BBC's *Songs of Praise* comes most weeks from Northern Ireland. According to the old cliché, when two complete strangers meet in Northern Ireland, the first thing one asks the other is a roundabout question to establish that person's denomination. Utter nonsense, of course — they would already know that.

In Southern Ireland, Catholicism is still the predominant force — that and horse-racing. Pilgrims come from far and wide to visit places associated with miracles, such as the airport at Knock. Visitors unversed in such matters should approach the whole subject with tact and discretion. Those that don't get put on the coach to Lough Derg.

Language

Irish (or Gaelic) is still preserved in special conversation areas, known as Gaeltachts (Gaeltachtaí), where people can say what they like about the visitors. As a language, Gaelic is generally considered to be too difficult, even for the Irish. Gaelic/Irish is officially the first language of the Republic, though most people have English, which is the second language, as their first language.

The Irish have a love of words, which is just as well in view of the complexities of Irish grammar (aspiration and eclipse change the beginnings of words and you may as well forget about plurals and endings).

LESSON ONE:

> Yes—*
> No—*
> *There is no yes or no in Irish.

LESSON TWO:

> Hello — Dia duit
>   — Dia daoibh
>   — Dia is Muire duit
> (depending on whether it's to one person or more, or said in reply)

ORAL PRACTICE (POLICE OFFICERS ONLY):

> Dia duit, Dia daoibh, Dia's Muire duit.

LESSON THREE:

> Slán agat — I give up.

IMPORTANT:

> Do not confuse the following —
> Shebeen/Skibbereen
> Poteen/Drisheen
> Crusheen/Smithereen
> Boreen/Colleen
> Noreen/Doreen
> Tureen/Carragheen
> Gombeen/Gurteen
> Baked bean/Bogbean

Pronunciation Class

A FEW WORDS OF IRISH
with translations into English

Literature & Arts

Ireland has no shortage of philosophers and original tinkers. ('Oi tink, therefore oi am.' Murphy's Law.) Jonathan Swift was an Irishman and so was the great Burke.

Ireland is a country with strong literary traditions — every town has its bookmaker. Lots of great writers have come out of Ireland: Goldsmith, Moore, Wilde, Joyce, Beckett ... In fact, very few ever chose to stay there.

Poets and playwrights are specialities of Ireland, with R B Sheridan, G B Shaw, W B Yeats, J M Synge and Sean O'Casey heading the list of men of letters. Nor should we forget such important female figures on the literary scene as Lady Augusta Gregory, Florence Court, Joyce O'Casey, Edna O'Brien ...

W.B. YEATS IN THE CELTIC TWILIGHT

"We're just here for a week to re-visit 'The Ould Sod' — "

It was Synge who outraged polite society by introducing *Playboy* to his Dublin audience. It went down a riot at the Abbey Theatre. The word 'shift' (as in 'scene-shifts') caused such commotion they had to send for Yeats to quell the troubles. These were the kind of petty pretensions which in turn drove Oscar Wilde.

Yeats himself is Ireland's greatest literary figure. Not only was he a poet and a playwright; he also managed to stay in Ireland for most of his life. Everyone knows the poem *Innisfree*, where the 'Nine bean rows thingy whatsit.. in the bee-loud glade'. Lovers of Yeats can follow his trail round Sligo — a leisurely tour for beginners and those who might not manage the Brendan Behan Trail round Dublin.

VISUAL ARTS

Celtic influences are strong in Irish art — endless patterns of intertwining loops and circles, ever-changing shapes in an infinite variety of forms. These are skills shared by the practitioners of other art-forms, such as the seanchaí (traditional story-teller) and the giver of road-directions. However, the tendency to twirl has been something of a handicap to modern artists, with Ireland scoring few successes in the worlds of Cubism or Post-Modern Minimalism.

Ireland has one great painter, the multi-talented Yeats, who painted under the name of Jack. Or sometimes John.

FILMS

Shooting in Ireland seems to appeal to film and television programme-makers everywhere. *Ryan's Daughter* was shot on the Dingle peninsula in authentic surroundings now dismantled. Stunning locations, perfect light and cheap local labour have attracted to Ireland many Hollywood producers out for pathos and a possible Oscar.

TELEVISION

The Irish facility with words is an invaluable asset in broadcasting, especially useful in times of cock-up and technical breakdown. The BBC has for so long depended upon the velvet voice of the Irish (Wogan, John Cole, Eamonn Andrews — and his famous sisters), that it would be hard to imagine switching on without tuning in to the soft lilt of an Irish rogue.

At home, broadcasting is in the hands of Radio Telefizz Eireann or RTE, which stands for Reception Terrible Everywhere.

Music & dance

Ireland has a thriving tradition of do-it-yourself enter-tainment, which dates back long before the days of tele-vision, radio or even Gay Byrne. Music in Ireland is a bit like breathing — something quite natural, something which happens all the time, something which other peo-ple tend to do down the back of your neck.

All over Ireland feet tap and buildings shake to the sound of traditional music on ancient instruments — fid-dle and pipe, whistle and spoons, rocking-chair, cardigan ... Add in the haunting wail of the uilleann pipes and the comforting beat of the bodhrán (made from a circular piece of goat stretched over beechwood) and you have all the ingredients for a memorable evening. Especially if you've paid for the room above.

Wherever you go in Ireland, look out for musical 'sessions'. These are completely impromptu and generally advertised in local newspapers. (But do remember they're only practising.) Watch out, too, for signs of Fleadh or Feis, the festivals of music and song, drink and dance that take place all summer in whichever place you're trying to drive through.

Traditional Irish dancing is a dangerous sport, involving breathtaking manoeuvres of the lower limbs. Competition can be cut-throat among the performers of jigs and reels, step and set-dances, but an atmosphere of friendly antagonism usually prevails.

Irish music has a huge following, thanks to bands like Clannad, The Chieftains, The Clancy Brothers, The Fureys … not forgetting The Dubliners, written about by Joyce.

Despite frequent successes in the Eurovision Song Contest, Ireland has a fine reputation for musical achievement. Not for nothing is the rock-bank U2 generally reckoned, in Ireland at least, the greatest in the world.

PENNY WHISTLE MUSIC :

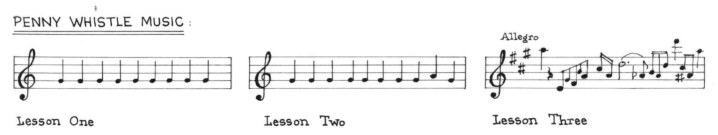

Lesson One   Lesson Two   Lesson Three

Sport

Historic divisions have tended to split Irish sport into two main categories. First there are the Gaelic Games — hurling, Gaelic football, camogie, road bowls and other bloodsports. Gaelic games have few rules (no tickling being the main one). Camogie is a form of hurling for women, played with shorter sticks and slightly smaller bruises. These sports are played mostly in the Republic, but teams from all over Ireland do take part in the Gaelic League (founded in the last century by Douglas Hurd).

In the second category come all remaining sports. Bridg-

Local pastime: harvesting seaweed.

ing the gap are boxing and rugby, two activities which do unite all elements in Ireland, enabling people from opposite sides of the fence to get together and beat the living daylights out of each other.

Golf is played all over Ireland, apart from the many lakes, which are paradise to coarse fishermen — and hell for golfers.

Ireland has produced world champions in a number of sports, from cycling to golf, hurling to snooker. Those who do scale the dizzy heights can expect to receive warm applause for their efforts, some even being offered premiership, royalty or just canonisation.

Horses

The Irish love horses and horses love Ireland. The grass is nowhere greener. Hunting and show-jumping have always been strong in Ireland, but it is racing which draws the biggest crowds, whether along the flat or over the sticks. The steeplechase is an Irish invention: in 1752 a Mr Blake raced a Mr O'Callaghan over 4 ½ miles of ditches, hedges and assorted washing-lines in County Cork, from Buttevant Church to the neighbouring spire of St Leger's. History does not record how the horses made it up the church tower.

Punchestown, Fairyhouse, Leopardstown, The Curragh … the names have a magical ring. No Irishman can resist a flutter — it's in his bloodstock and breeding. Backing dead certs every time, the Irish lose a fortune on the horses. This is known as the luck of the Irish.

Racing is a serious business, but there are some fun occasions, such as the annual race of Hospital Sweeps, impressive all in black.

White horses!

IRISH BEACH HAZARDS

Breeding takes up much time and energy in Ireland. Interested visitors can pop in to the National Stud in Kildare, where soft music is played to the mares (upset, no doubt, by the nearby presence of Arkle's skeleton).

Another firm favourite with visitors is a traditional Horse Fair, like that at Spancil Hill, with its colourful language and picturesque scenes of trading and barter. In line with ancient ritual, prices are haggled over with rising indignation till suddenly a deal is struck, by spitting on the palms, and sealed with a friendly handshake — something you'll no doubt wish to try for yourself when buying an ice-cream or hamburger. Get the right person, though, or you may find you've bought a horse instead.

'soft music is played to the mares...'

Shaggy but rugged, the Connemara Pony...

Touring Ireland

Getting There

sea bird . . . Sea Cat .

Those wishing to fly by Irish airlines can choose between Ryanair and its state-owned rival, wittily known as Aer Fungus. At sea there is choice of routes operated by B & I, P & O etc. to get you from A to B. There are regular sailings between Stranraer and Larne, Cairnryan and Larne, Holyhead and Dun Laoghaire (pronounced Dun-thingy), Larne and Stranraer, Roscoff and Cork, Cork and Rosslare ... At every port of entry you will find jaunting-cars ready and waiting to whisk you to your hotel or holiday destination.

DRIVING IN IRELAND

The speed-limit in the Republic is 55 mph (88 kph), with 30 mph (48 kph) restrictions in built-up areas. This sensible limit, which applies also to donkeys and horse-drawn vehicles, is aimed principally at giving motorists time to read the signposts. The speed-limit applies to all roads in the Republic, including motorways. The Republic has no motorway-network as such, but an extensive support-system of smaller roads, affectionately known as 'dual cabbageways'.

In Northern Ireland newly-qualified drivers must in their first year drive with plates marked 'R', which stands for 'reckless'.

SIGNPOSTS

Travel in the Republic can be confusing as almost every place has two different names (one Irish, one English) and almost every name occurs in two different places. Often more. If in doubt, don't ask a local.

Irish signposts serve one main purpose: ensuring that incomers are headed off down long-forgotten tracks whose layout clearly owes something to the Book of Kells. In the event of invasion, far from removing all direction-signs, the Irish Army has secret orders to move swiftly about the countryside checking that signposts are clearly visible and all in order.

Distances in the Republic are usually given in English miles or kilometres. The Irish mile is 2240 yards, which is 480 yards more than the English (which is 1.60934 kilometres).

Before visiting Ireland, motorists should familiarise themselves with the following:

 Two cars stopped in road ahead to let drivers discuss the state of the universe

 Park here at an angle across the continuous line

 Slow down

 Goal posts in need of repair

 Watch out for sharp rise in petrol prices

 Welcome to the lakes of Fermanagh

 Can't you read eejit?

 Your car is about to take off

 Traditional story-teller ahead

 Road Bowling in progress round next bend

 I give up

 Child-molester ahead

 Inadvisable to stop here and ask for directions

 Dubious Bed & Breakfast ahead

 Parking area

 Double-parking area

Suggested Tours

TOUR ONE

From Jack's Hole in Wicklow, pass through Sally Gap and drive north to Rostrevor. Call in on Annalong and Bessbrook, before heading west through Jamestown and Claremorris into Joyce's Country. From the Twelve Bens drive south past Garrykennedy, Nenagh and Clare on your way to Kerry. See Moll's Gap, but don't let Tim Healy Pass by until you're ready.

TOUR TWO

From Dublin's harbour-mouth at Howth head north to Dowth and Knowth, just south of Louth.

TOUR THREE

(Adults only)

Start from Blacksod Bay and drive east (the only blooming way possible). Hours later you should reach Ballysodare, half-way to Bloody Foreland. If not wholly fed up by now, head south-east across Ulster, looking for the Bloody Bridge near Newcastle. Continue south. Eventually you should find the Termonfeckin road.

IRISH PLACENAMES EXPLAINED

ATH means ford as in Athlone, Athlumney, Athletic, Athleague ...

BALLINA means ford as in Ballinaboola, Ballinamuck, Ballinspittle, Dripsey, Spiddle and Spink ...

BALLY means town as in Ballyboggan, Ballygalley, Galbally, Ballyhooley, Oola, Bohola, Boho ...

BUN means foot or mouth as in Bundoran, Buncrana, Buncurrant, Bunbeg, Bunratty, Bunmole, Bunmixture ...

CLON means meadow as in Clonkeen, Clonca, Clonakilty, Clonegal, Donegal, Donnylonegan, Monaghan, Finnegan, Chinnigan ...

DERRY means oak-grove as in Derrydonnell, Derrybeg, Derrydown, Merrydown, Heydown, Hoedown, Derryderrydown ...

DRUM means hillock as in Drumbo, Drumfree, Drumbilla, Drumbeatin, Drumshanbo ...

DUFF means black as in Ballyduff, Clonduff, Lugduff, Plumduff ...

DUN means fort as in Dungiven, Dunlavin, Dunroamin, Dundaniel, Dundanion, Dundandelion ...

FORD means ford as in Ford ...

GLEN menas glen as in Glenford, Glencampbell, Glenarm, Glenariff, Glengarriff, Glendoo, Glendalough, Glendajackson, Glendun ...

LIS means earth-fort (see Rath) as in Lisdoonvarna, Liscarrol, Listaylor, Lismore, Lornadoon ...

KNOCK means hill as in Knockbrit, Knockboy, Knockma, Knockmoy, Knockmany, Knockknock, Knockalongy, Knocknee ...

NEW means old as in Newgrange, Newcastle, Newtown, Newmarket, New Shopping Centre ...

RATH means earth-fort (see Liss) as in Rathmullen, Rathmore, Rathmichael, Rathdrum, Rathole, Rathvilly ...

TULLY means hillock as in Tullygallen, Tullaghoge, Tullynally, Tallyho, Tallow, Tullow, Hullo, Mallow, Allo, Aberlow, Athlone, Athlumney, Athleague ...

Where to stay

Hospitable by nature, the Irish think nothing of an extra guest at the table. The B & B sign is regarded in most homes as an essential piece of garden furniture. Accommodation is usually in the traditional Irish homestead, a ranch-type bungalow, heavily modelled on Dallas.

The more discerning may prefer the Big Houses and historic castles where guests can pay that little bit extra to stay in ancient beds with lots of atmosphere. At the cheaper end of the range are ordinary homes with simple arrangements, to which visitors are heartily welcome.

Many first-time visitors to Ireland cherish the notion of staying in a genuine, traditional thatched cottage from days of yore. There are plenty such places to be had, pictured in holiday brochures. Dream-cottages they seem in the photos, but do check, when you make your booking, that all is as it should be inside. The real Irish cottage is a one-roomed cabin, half given over to animals, with sod roof and walls constructed of turf (easy to bang a nail in, but hard to hang a picture).

'The place we're staying in is just yards from the sea . . .'

...and not another soul on the road!

ON THE ROAD

Lots of visitors play safe by taking their accommodation with them. You'll have seen the many caravanners drawn up by the sides of the road.

Cruising the inland waterways in an option especially popular with Europeans nervous of driving on the left. Rules of the river are fairly straightforward: keep to the right and try to remember that Upper Lough Erne is below Lower Lough Erne on the map — except when the map is turned.

Finally, what could beat the horse-drawn caravan! This gentle and relaxing mode of transport gives time to appreciate Ireland's grand views, slowly changing above the horse's bottom. As a means of travel, the horse-drawn caravan is 'environment-friendly', but watch out for noxious emissions from the horse's exhaust. Bathroom facilities on caravans are generally limited and halts in the wild, treeless landscape of Connemara are often dictated by the need for cover. Expect to do about ten miles a day, on a route that is chosen by the horse.

SOUVENIR IDEAS

Address book — ask for the Irish edition, with enlarged 'O' section.

Aran jersey — with distinctive pattern, designed to help identify bodies long at sea that are washed ashore. Useful for the ferry home.

Irish crochet — with lawn appliqué. Mallets and ball come separately.

Irish lace — beautifully made, though not much use for doing up shoes. Lace handkerchiefs are always popular, though bad news for heavy colds.

Irish linen — worth just giving those hankies a sniff in the shop to make sure they carry the genuine smell of Ulster flax (retted, hackled and scutched by hand) and are not some cheap and nasty foreign import.

Irish racehorse — check it's not Shergar.

Irish whiskey — try a bottle of old Bushmills (made in

BELLEEK SOUP BOWL

1608) — or you may prefer to ask if they've anything newer tucked under the counter.

Pampooties — traditional Aran Island footwear. Bear in mind these need to be dipped in seawater every three hours to prevent the rawhide from drying out and chafing uncomfortably.

Penny whistle — available from most tourist outlets at around IR£2-10.

Religious items — watch out for moving statues and the odd bargain to be found in the Sales (such as a dodgy Saint or slightly soiled Virgin).

Shamrock — be sure to get the real thing (though no one's quite sure which of four plants that is).

Waterford Glass — don't be afraid to ask if you might rummage among the seconds for something a little cheaper …

… and, if all else fails, you should find no shortage of colourful knick-knacks, produced by Irish emigrants in the Far East, who do amusing things with leprechauns.

CLADDAGH RING
traditionally worn by heart-transplant surgeons in rural Galway.

Food

Often written off as staid and uninteresting, Irish cuisine is well up to springing a surprise or two upon the unwary, as those who order the Full Irish Breakfast soon discover. Ulster bacon is known for its high quality, while a hearty portion of drisheen (black pudding) will soon get you going in the morning.

Ireland is in the throes of a gastro-renaissance. Food and Drink Festivals take place most weeks in Ireland and any food writer in danger of going short in between can always make the pilgrimage to Ballymaloe.

Beef and dairy products are big in Ireland. Irish cattle farmers deserve a pat on the back for their notable contributions to the European Beef and Butter Mountains. Cheeses go back a long way in Ireland, with local preferences clearly favouring the firmer varieties. (Queen Maeve was actually killed by a piece of cheese, fired by her nephew with his sling. If only she'd packed the Brie …) With a wide range of new traditional cheeses now being produced, best-known native cheeses are still Irish Cheddar and Irish Gorgonzola.

Edible Crab
wishing it had
another name.

50

Pacific oysters, salmon well poached (or lawfully obtained), Lough Neagh eel, Dublin Bay prawn (or Norway lobster), brown trout, cockles and mussels ... Seafood and fish are available in such abundance that in Ireland salmon and oysters have come to be regarded as poor man's fare, to be palmed off abroad.

The subject of vegetables is something of a haute potato in Irish culinary circles. Greens feature in all walks of life in Ireland, except on the dinner-plate. The humble potato has traditionally outshone all other veg. in the dish. Changes are beginning to take place with the arrival of nouvelle cuisine ('novel kitchen'), showing just what interesting things can be done with one stick of celery and two small peas.

The Irish still eat 141 kilos (22 stone or five and a half sacks) of spuds per person per year.

I'm just a sole whose intentions are good...

ULSTER FRY ['Olsta Fray']

The glory of Irish cookery is its home baking. Barm brack, soda bread, shortbread, Guinness cake, tipsy cake, wheaten farls ... small wonder that the Northern Irish have a reputation for solidity. The Ulsterman's stomach is close to his heart and who could blame him.

What exiled Ulster folk miss most of all is the province's legendary baking. A certain amount slips out, smuggled in suitcases (bun-running), to the natural concern of the authorities. Such is the yearning abroad for Veda Bread that the security forces have had to step up their vigilance at airports and even consider the introduction of sniffer-ducks at Aldergrove.

To end on a happier note, a sample menu from the heart of Ireland -

Starters
Stuffed Avoca
Sperrins
or Potato

Main Course
Flan O'Brien
Belmullet or Belturbet
Kilcock (in season)
or Potato

Sweet Trolley
Apple Crumlin
Great Sugar Loaf
Oven-fresh Macrooms or
sticky chunk of fresh Bunclody
or Potato

The countryside is well-supplied with picnic-tables

... And drink

Ireland's national drink is Guinness. The precious black liquid rises from a natural borehole in a secret location near Dublin, whence it is piped across the country. The capital is named after this natural wonder (Dubhlinn means 'dark pool'). Other sacred wells (Murphy's and Beamish) exist in the region of Cork, their precise whereabouts guarded by the Church.

Drawing a pint of Guinness is a special skill, acquired

IRISH BARS ARE FAMOUS FOR THEIR CONVIVIALITY

only through years of training, night-school and rigorous examinations. Only the elite are called to the bar.

The properly pulled stout has a head that a mouse could run across. The pint must then be allowed to sit in silence, entirely unmolested, to gather its strength for two and three-quarter minutes. (Don't embarrass those around you by speaking during this critical stage.) To ensure that standards are always maintained, plain-clothes inspectors do the rounds of Ireland's pubs, measuring the head on a pint and testing its consistency. It's fun to spot a senior, mouse-carrying inspector: watch out for the tell-tale wriggle in the trouser-pocket and a certain edginess in the presence of cats.

Ireland's other drink is Scotch, known as Irish, because

10p sized blob of froth remains attached to nose-tip for minimum 12 seconds

THE CORRECTLY PULLED STOUT

'A friendly rivalry...'

they invented it. Irish whiskey is noted for its pronounced flavour and peculiar spelling. Scotch whisky and Irish whiskey are really two quite different drinks, miles apart in origin and character. One has an 'e' in it and the other doesn't. A friendly rivalry exists between the two schools of whisk(e)y-drinking.

54

The way of life

Travel and increased mobility have meant that Ireland today is populated by a veritable mixture of types, unimaginable in former times. O'Malleys have married O'Driscolls, McGrottys mated up with McGurks and Flanagans gone off with the Shanahans. It's something of a rarity nowadays to see a proper Irishman, with his red hair, short temper and telltale shillelagh. Or harp, if female.

However, all is not lost. Old ways survive beneath the slick veneer of modern living. Time (2 ½ days behind Greenwich Mean Time) still goes slowly. Life is relaxed and leisurely. Ancient traditions are kept up in colourful country rituals, like dancing at Lughnasa, hunting the wren and burning down half the street in July.

IRISH ATTITUDES

Friendly by nature, the Irish prefer conviviality and good cheer to sitting things out in sober isolation. On Scottish islands, it has been noted, settlement takes place on the public-urinal system, each newcomer politely moving into the spot most distant from everyone else. Cottages are scattered far and wide. On Irish islands, by contrast, homesteads cluster in chummy huddles of tight togetherness.

Talking in Ireland is a national pastime. Sudden disappearance of the hind-legs is a source of constant worry to Irish donkeys. Expert talkers delight in leading the listener down tortuous tracks and off into flights of pure fancy. Just settle back and enjoy the 'crack'!

Irishmen everywhere are famous for 'The Crack'.

55

Gazetteer

Dublin

Dublin, which means 'Blackpool', was founded on Guinness by Vikings. A favourite with all ages today is The Irish Life Viking Adventure, which, with its recreation of authentic Viking sounds and smells (bludgeoning and pillage extra, by arrangement), leaves a lasting impression on visitors.

The city began on 1st January 988. It has recently celebrated its millennium. In 1991 Dublin was hailed as a city of culture, but has now reverted to its old Philistine ways (except around Dublin 4 and the bars of the Shelbourne Hotel).

Early Dubliner

MOLLY MALONE

GETTING AROUND

Getting about Dublin is quite straightforward, once you've mastered the city's parallel ring-roads and simple-to-follow system of traffic-lights. When it comes to public transport, the visitor is spoilt for choice, from open-top bus to gentle gondola, skimming the azure surface of Dublin's Grand Canal. Taxis are plentiful and not hard to spot, though visitors from abroad frequently make the mistake of hailing the gardaí instead. Do not be discouraged to find most buses bound for the busy district of Baile Atha Cliath — there's sure to be one for Dublin along in a minute.

Whether you choose to stretch out in College Green or simply sit and relax by the limpid waters of the Liffey (tributaries the Dodder and the Poddle), Dublin's centre is a place of gentle calm. Here it is the easiest thing in the world to pass half the day on a traffic island, just watching the world go by. The more active may prefer to walk the streets, in the footsteps of Dublin's most famous resident, Molly Malone ('the tart with the cart').

DUBLIN DOORS ARE JUSTLY FAMOUS, IF SOMEWHAT CLOSE TOGETHER

THINGS TO SEE

There's something for everyone in Dublin, from Nelson's head in the Civic Museum to feeding-time for the rare phoenix in the world's second oldest privately-owned zoo. Sacred monuments include Christ Church Cathedral (with heart of Peter O'Toole), St Patrick's Cathedral (with rended heart of Jonathan Swift, as well as roof made out of shillelaghs) and, of course, the Guinness Museum.

Most tourists choose to saunter over Halfpenny Bridge (have coins ready in advance) and pick their way carefully up Grafton Street, trying to avoid being stung by buskers on the way. From here it is but a short stroll on to Trinity College and its famous library. Follow the signs round to a main entrance packed out with visitors lining up to view the priceless treasures within -- the Library Shop is always a popular stop on the Dublin Trail. Above it is the Long Room, housing the world-famous illuminated Book of Kells (just ask for it to be switched on, if not already lit). Alongside are the Book of Durrow and only slightly less well illuminated Book of Dimma. Nearby is the remarkable 500 year-old harp made for Brian Boru, who died in 1014.

Open·top bus

Province of Leinster

Ireland has 5 provinces — Leinster, Munster, Connacht, Ulster and Liverpool. First-time visitors arriving from Britain may find much of Leinster (Ireland's south-eastern quarter) somewhat disappointing, with its prosperous bungalows and absence of donkeys. Tourists in search of the Real Ireland should drive straight on to Killarney.

COUNTY DUBLIN

Co Dublin has an interesting coastline dotted with Martello Towers. These were built to prevent Napoleon from invading Ireland. They were most successful.

Best-known resident of a Martello Tower is James Joyce, who lived in one for a week. Dublin is famous for all the great writers who left the city. James Joyce is Dublin's favourite son — his works were banned by the city long after his death. Nowadays they are readily obtainable; newcomers to Joyce should ask for the English translations of his work.

he capital and its environs are served principally y DART (the Dublin Area Rapid Transit system).

HAVING A BAD MORNING IN KELLS

COUNTY MEATH

Co Meath is the home ground for Irish History. From the first slurpings of the Beaker Folk to the fateful Battle of the Boyne, almost all Ireland's great events have been played out in Meath. The county brims with ancient sites and monuments — Newgrange, Knowth, Dowth, the Hill of Tara, Kells, Trim … not forgetting the Hill of Slane, where Patrick lit the Paschal Fire.

Beaker Folk

COUNTY WESTMEATH

Westmeath has the exact centre of Ireland, marked by a hill-tower near Glassan. Other dead-centres are marked by Hodson's Pillar on an island in Lough Ree, the Cat Stone near Mullingar and at Birr in Co Offaly. Westmeath is cattle-raising country.

COUNTY LOUTH

The 'wee county' of Louth is steeped in myth and rich in ruins. The legendary Cuchulainn was born at Castletown and lived in Dundalk. Mortally wounded in the GPO at Dublin, he died in Louth, strapped to the standing stone at Clochafermor. Nearby is the Cooley Peninsula, setting of the 'Cattle Raid of Cooley', a fantastic tale too often dismissed as a load of old bull.

Local industries include brewing, tobacco and the conversion of potatoes into alcohol.

Cattle-raising country

COUNTY KILDARE

Co Kildare is home to The Curragh and a land where the racehorse is king. At the heart of Kildare is The National Stud, which members of the public can visit to see horses breeding. The whole county is dotted with studs and seminaries, which should not be muddled.

COUNTY OFFALY

Offaly, like all its neighbours, is distinguished by its fine bogs, small towns, ancient ruins and vague claim to the exact centre of Ireland. Clonmacnoise, along the Shannon, is not so much an historic site as a veritable pile-up, with the crashed remains of eight churches and one cathedral scattered about for a start.

Downstream lies Banagher, where Trollope wrote his early novels while working as a post-office clerk. This can't have been much fun for those lined up on the other side of the counter.

Coarse Fish

COUNTY LONGFORD

Co Longford, flat and green, is an area of coarse fish and literary pilgrimage. Fans of Oliver Goldsmith flock here to visit the places where he was born (Pallas in Longford and Elphin in Roscommon). Mostrim, or Edgeworthstown for short, is well-known for its associations with the celebrated Edgeworths, famous for their connections with the town.

JUST HALF AN HOUR'S DRIVE OUT OF DUBLIN, THE WICKLOW MOUNTAINS

DUAL · CARRIAGEWAY IN IRELAND

COUNTY WICKLOW

No distance at all from the centre of Dublin — just an inch on the map — is lovely Wicklow with its gaps and mountains. Chief attractions are Powerscourt ('the Garden of Ireland') and tranquil Glendalough, long the haunt of hermits, scholars and coach-parties seeking solitude.

COUNTY LAOIS

Portlaoise (sometimes spelt 'Maryborough') is the county town of low-flying Laois or Leix (pronounced 'Queen's County' or 'Leesh'). Notable sights are the round towers of Timahoe and Portarlington. High over these soar the Slieve Bloom Mountains, one of which reaches right up to 1,734 feet.

Avoca, Meeting of the Waters.

COUNTY CARLOW

Co Carlow, at the foot of the Backstairs, is a small county with rolling hills and twisting roads — even by Irish standards. At its centre stand the few remains of Carlow Castle, which withstood many sieges in its time, only to be blasted apart by an over-enthusiastic D-I-Y man in 1814. Making space for replacement windows to go in his proposed lunatic asylum, Dr Middleton overshot on gunpowder.

Close by is Browne's Hill Dolmen, whose 100 ton capstone (regularly weighed) is still the heaviest in Europe.

COUNTY KILKENNY

Kilkenny was once capital of Ireland. The Normans, who were very big here, left behind bits of castle and abbey all over the place. Knocktopher, for example, has a medieval tower and doorway still standing, though most of the priory alongside is now knocked over.

In 1366 Parliament passed the infamous Statues of Kilkenny. These penalised Normans for hibernating with the natives.

COUNTY WEXFORD

Wexford, in the bottom right-hand corner of Ireland, is a county of long sandy beaches and gentle landscapes, which have witnessed more than their share of savagery. Cromwell is not forgotten, nor are Vinegar Hill and the 1798 Uprising. However, present-day visitors are made heartily welcome, especially bird-spotting opera-buffs who know their seafood.

BIKING IN WICKLOW

LIFE ON THE SKELLIGS WAS TOUGH

Province of Munster

T he west of Ireland is a region of wild coasts and rugged peninsulas, peopled only by homesick Americans patiently waiting for that magical glimpse of distant skyscraper through the mist.

COUNTY WATERFORD

Co Waterford, in the sun-drenched south-east of Ireland, is a place of grand strands (Tramore, Stradbally, Bunmahon) and modest mountains (Comeraghs, Monavullaghs and Knockmealdowns). The city of Waterford was founded by Vikings, notably Reginald, son of Sigtryg and next-door neighbour of Blogstik, Thangwyn and Betty.

Knockmealdown with a feather

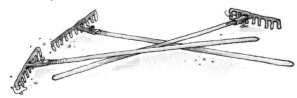

Rakes of Mallow

COUNTY CORK

Cork is Ireland's largest county. It starts at Youghal (pronounced 'Yawl'), where Sir Walter Raleigh (pron. 'Rawley') first chewed tobacco in Europe (pron. 'Yawrp') and puffed on a potato. To the north is fertile Mallow, a centre for sugar-beet and famous for its rakes.

Cork City is 'the Paris of Ireland' and each June its Cannes. Watch out in summer for bottlenecks round Cork. 'Rebel Cork' has a reputation for stubbornness and guile, qualities shared by all Corkmen and women (or 'corkers', as they're generally known).

Close to Cork is Blarney Castle with its much-loved Stone, which is Ireland's single greatest tourist attraction. A quick dangle over the battlements makes it possible for the gift of the gob to be transferred from visitor to visitor. The Blarney Stone is scrubbed with disinfectant four times a day.

COUNTY KERRY

Englishmen laugh at Irishmen; Irishmen laugh at Kerrymen and Kerrymen laugh to the bank. Kerry is a place of stupendous beauty. Unpronounceable mountains rise over the ragged bulwarks of Beara, Iveragh and Dingle. Offshore loom deserted islands, such as the Skelligs, where monks once clung to the cliffs, and the Blaskets, inhabited by writers till 1953.

At Killorglin each August a wild goat is crowned king for 3 days and hoisted high over the town square; anyone beneath stands the chance of further anointment.

Northwards lies the important rose-growing district of Tralee.

Gallarus Oratory, Co. Kerry
in which Brendan first sailed to America   71

THE WEST OF IRELAND IS FAMOUS FOR ITS COLOUR

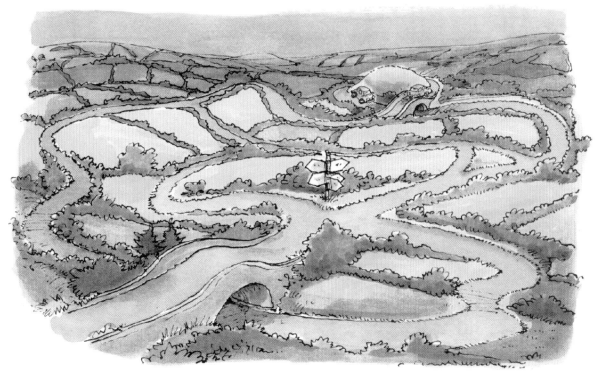

IRISH ROAD SYSTEM

COUNTY LIMERICK

Limerick is best-known for ham and rude verse. Mostly low-lying, the county rises up at its edges, except along the Shannon. Seefin, the highest point of the Ballyhouras, is capped by a cairn marking the grave of Finn MacCool's poet son Ossian, who also lies buried near Cushendall in Antrim.

A footpath over the Ballyhouras is part of the O'Sullivan Beara Walk, a long distance trail which traces the route of the fleeing chieftain in the winter of 1602/3. He left Bantry Bay with a thousand followers, only 34 of whom survived the epic march with him to Leitrim over fourteen grim days. To cross the Shannon they were forced to eat their horses, using the skins to make a curragh. Present-day travellers should try for the ferry at Tarbert.

THE INVENTION OF THE LIMERICK

COUNTY TIPPERARY

Co Tipperary is large and varied and, as most people like to point out, a long way to go. The town of Tipperary is not the county town of County Tipperary, which is Clonmel (almost outside the county) instead.

Tipperary's natural wonders and chief historical attractions include the Rock of Cashel, the Glen of Aherlow, the Galtee Mountains, the Golden Vale and the Ronald Reagan pub in Ballyporeen.

Ballyporeen – ancestral home of the Reagans

Armada wreck

COUNTY CLARE

Co Clare has something for everyone — Doolin for music-lovers, Ennistymon for its shop-fronts and the Cliffs of Moher to frighten the pants off anyone nervous of heights. Out to sea are the Aran Islands, first discovered in 1898 by J M Synge. A little way inland is the spa town of Lisdoonvarna, popular for its radioactive waters and well-known match-factory. Best of all is The Burren with its lunar landscape and strange species lurking in the rocky crevices. Try stepping on a crack in the limestone pavement and see for yourself.

THE MAKINGS OF A NASTY INCIDENT IN THE BURREN

GOATS ON THE CLIFFS OF MOHER

Province of Connacht

Beautiful Connaught is The Wild West of Ireland, where damp hills surround vast tracts of empty bogland. Only golf-courses, seaweed-eating ponies and interpretive centres can survive the rigours of the climate and harshness of this terrain.

Great Moments in History:
1919. Alcock and Brown crash-land in Derrygimlagh Bog.

COUNTY GALWAY

Flat and tame for the first bit, Co Galway goes wild after Galway City. Beyond Lough Corrib is Connemara, much haunted by calendar photographers. The Twelve Bens (or Pins) have lilting Gaelic names: Binn Gabhar, An Mhaoileann, An Cailleach, Binn Leitrí, Magairle … These lose something in translation: The Goat, The Bald, The Hag, The Spewy Slopes, Somebody's Testicle …

Galway City is lively and cosmopolitan — Christopher Columbus was a regular visitor. The city straddles the River Corrib. An angler's dream, the Salmon Weir Bridge is where the fish line up in springtime, positively begging to be hooked. Arts events and cultural activities take place throughout the year, notably The Races in August, the Oyster Festivals in September and The Hangover in October. Galway Bay, where the sun goes down, is a pleasant spot to stroll along at any time, keeping an eye out for Galway Hookers heading your way.

COUNTY MAYO

The coastline of Mayo is a place of awesome beauty for visitors — and sheer hell for mapmakers. Place-names are a particular hazard: try Killary's 'Cooneenashkirroogohifrinn' for starters. (Don't be afraid to ask for the extra long envelopes held in stock by local stationers.) Clew Bay is dotted with innumerable small islands — 365 altogether, plus one which appears every fourth year.

Beyond Clew lie Achill and Clare, former island strongholds of 16th century pirate-queen Grace O'Malley ('The Granule'). TERRA MARIQUE POTENS reads the motto on her memorial tablet ('a mighty terror to both her husbands').

Gazetteer: CONNACHT

OYSTER FESTIVAL

WEDGE-TOMB

COUNTY SLIGO

Heavily overpopulated in ancient times, Co Sligo is thickly spread with megalithic remains — Carrowmore, Carrowkeel, Creevykeel, Creevycrawley ... Overlooking Sligo Town (home of solicitors Argue & Phibbs) is the large hill of Knocknarea, topped by Maeve's Graeve. The much-buried Maeve, who has a second tomb on Knockma in Galway, is believed to lie at rest at Rathcroghan (Roscommon).

North of Sligo Town are the Dartry Mountains, on whose slopes Diarmuid was slain by a bore. Below is Drumcliff, where Yeats lies buried 'under bare Ben Bulben's head'. The whole of Sligo is now known as Yeats Country, thanks to the many pubs and bars named after him. Each year Sligo plays host to the Yeats Summer School, where poetry enthusiasts meet to thrash out the questions of the day, viz. Who was Bare Ben Bulben? What happened to the rest of him? and What rhymes with Sligo?

FISHING OFF MAYO

WHY THEY BUILT DOLMENS

COUNTY LEITRIM

Co Leitrim, the well-known mapping error, ends up with just 2 ½ miles of coastline and a whopping great lake right across its middle. Lough Allen, with resident monster, chops the county in two.

Leitrim's county town is Carrick, a place whose sleepy calm is broken only by the sounds of mutinous crew on visiting hire-craft.

Fishing on Lough Gara

COUNTY ROSCOMMON

The mighty O'Connors of Roscommon provided 24 Kings of Connacht and enough High Kings of Ireland to form a football team, though they'd have to make do without subs. The lakes of Roscommon are well stocked with fish and archaeological treasures — more than 30 dug-out boats have been fished out of Lough Gara alone.

Province of Ulster

U lster is the bit everyone knows about. Or thinks they do. Planter territory, the region is scattered with small towns formed round triangular squares called Diamonds.

Reckoned to be more taciturn and restrained, Ulster folk have a turn of phrase every bit as colourful as their southern neighbours. Read yer man John Pepper for further elucidation, right enough.

COUNTY MONAGHAN

Monaghan, which means 'Little Hills', consists entirely of small hills, some too small for the naked eye. Even the lakes have small hills in them. This is Gremlin Country.

COUNTY CAVAN

Cavan ('Cabhan', hollow place — or cavern) is named after the state of its roads. Regular winner in the National Worst Pothole Competition, Cavan's highway system boasts cracks and hollows which are explored by visiting potholers.

The songwriter Percy French was for some time Inspector of Drains with Cavan County Council, in which post he was inspired to write 'Come back, Paddy Reilly, to Ballyjamesduff' and 'Abdulla Bulbul Ameer'.

Cavan is O'Reilly territory. Finn MacCool's Fingers mark the spot where clan chiefs were inaugurated and the site of Cavan Abbey is where Slasher O'Reilly now lies interred

COUNTY DONEGAL

The coastline of Donegal weaves a wonderful course from sandy Bundoran round to windswept Malin, well-known from shipping-forecasts. Traditional ways live on in Donegal — handloom-weaving, fiddle-playing and the luring of tourists into craft-shops. Ireland's north-west corner is famous for flecked tweed jackets, woollen scarves, chunky home-knit sweaters and similar beachwear.

Off the coast of Donegal is Tory Island, which has a thriving community of naive artists, woodcarvers and makers of unusual souvenirs. There are no scheduled ferry-services and the local boatman will be happy to delay your return to the mainland until purchases have been made.

Northern Ireland

Haugh-ey
Haugh-ey

Portstewart Strand

Northern Ireland

COUNTY LONDONDERRY

Co Derry (the 'London-' is usually silent) boasts fine strands and fresh sea-breezes. Summer visitors flock here to sniff the Londonderry air (or 'London bottom' as it's known to the French). Danny Boy, the Londonderry heir, came from Limavady.

Derry itself, the 'Maiden City', is known for its fine-looking young women, whose walls have never been breached.

Along the north coast are the twin resorts of Portstewart (parking below the strand) and Portrush. Their quiet back roads play host each May to North-West 200, the fastest motorcycle races in the British Isles and bad news for hedgehogs.

COUNTY TYRONE

'Tyrone among the Bushes' takes a pride in its links with successful Americans. More than a dozen US presidents are of Ulster descent, not to mention Davy Crockett.

Tyrone's unspoilt landscape is gentle and mild, though fresh north-easterlies can make it draughty round the Sperrins. East of Cookstown (famous for sausages) is the great Lough Neagh, richly stocked with eel and midge (also known as Lough Neagh fly).

Lough Neagh fly

COUNTY FERMANAGH

Fermanagh is the 'Lakeland of Ulster'. Upper Lough Erne, with its maze of small islands, is a place where you can cruise in solitude for hours, getting thoroughly lost. Ditto Lower Lough Erne. Between the two is Enniskillen, built across a waterway well churned by lost cruisers.

In an overgrown cemetery on Boa Island stands the ancient two-faced idol sometimes cited as evidence of Britain's long involvement in Irish affairs. Nearby attractions include Castle Caldwell with its birds (Erne terns), Castle Coole with its 300 year-old greylag geese, Monea Castle and busy Marble Arch.

Carving the idol on Boa Island

87

COUNTY ARMAGH

Armagh is 'The Orchard of Ireland', famous for apples and citrus fruit. Ulster's Orangemen are known the whole world over. The city of Armagh has been ecclesiastical capital of Ireland since the 5th century, when St Patrick built a church here on a hill. St Patrick's Cathedral stands on another hill, on the site of the second church he built here. Overlooking it, on a nearby hill, are the twin spires of St Patrick's Cathedral. A few miles off to the south-east is Gosford Castle, built by the Normans in 1819.

COUNTY DOWN

Co Down (pronoynced Coynty Doyn) has many delights, including Strangford and the Ards, Downpatrick and the Quoile, Newcastle and the Mournes. Strangford Lough is a birdwatcher's paradise with its many small islands (formed from drowned dunlins). Newcastle's fine strand is where local inventor and pioneer airman Harry Ferguson first flew his famous tractor. Behind are the Mountains of Mourne, forever sweeping down to the sea. The Mourne Wall, 8 feet high and 22 miles long, was erected at the beginning of the century in a bid to hold the Mournes in place. At the heart of the mountains is Silent Valley with its two great reservoirs and almighty plughole, which is one of the premier attractions of Ulster.

Premier attraction . . .

The Vanishing Lake . . .

COUNTY ANTRIM

Co Antrim is known for its glens and even better known for its coastline. From Black Head and The Gobbins on Island Magee (beware no ferry services) the Antrim Coast sweeps round to Dunluce through a succession of splendours: Portmuck, Drains Bay, Kenbane, Benbane, not forgetting theatrical Larrybane ... Fair Head gives fine views over Rathlin and the Waters of Moyle (Scotland just 13 moyles). The precipitous Grey Man's Path drops 600 feet on to the rocks below (return by inshore rescue or lifeboat). Not far off, somewhere or other is Loughareema (or sometimes Loughaveema), the vanishing lake. Beyond Carrick-a-Rede is Whitepark Bay, much used in neolithic times.

Next along is the Giant's Causeway, major wonder and an inspiration to pencil-manufacturers the whole world over: 40,000 columns of stone (give or take those swiped for local patios), cunningly joined with barely a crack between them. What's more, they've all got names. Follow way-marked paths to the Chimney Tops, trying not to stare too obviously at The Giant's Organ on your way.

Whitepark Bay, much used in neolithic times...

91

Belfast

Orangeman
out celebrating

The city of Belfast lies at the head of Belfast Lough, stubbornly defying the various bids made to dislodge it. Hemmed in by hills, 'the Hibernian Rio' enjoys a distinctive skyline. Highest point is Cave Hill, capped by MacArt's Fort (pronounced with care).

Below, where the 'Lagan stream sings lullaby' into the lough, are Belfast's mighty shipyards, towered over by massive goalposts erected for the lunchtime recreation of the workforce.

Textiles (notably linen, poplin and crimplene) have provided the city with its other main source of wealth. Belfast ('No Surrender') is world-famous for white handkerchiefs.

All too often in the news, Belfast is a place of large parks and leafy suburbs, few of which ever make it on to the main bulletins. Recent years have seen the construction of a major motorway system to separate off the mainly Catholic and predominantly Prodestant areas of the city. (Drivers of other denominations should stick firmly to the centre-lane at all times.)

Famous Belfast folk include Harlandandwolff the shipbuilder, James Galway the flautist and Ian Paisley the well-known person.

THINGS TO DO

Busy Belfast offers plenty for the tourist, from lofty Balmoral, with all its royal associations, to the steamy ravines of the Botanic Gardens, where visitors can come and look at bananas. Or try the underwater viewing of sealions and penguins at Belfast Zoo (change of clothing advisable). Not far off is Carrickfergus Castle with its historic fibre-glass figures; out to the east is Hollywood (or 'Tinseltown'), which always draws its share of inquisitive visitors.

It's the way they look at you with those beady eyes –

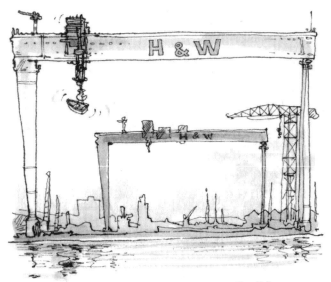

Hard times for Belfast shipbuilders

CITY STROLL

Starting on the north-west corner of the City Hall in Donegall Square, head east into Donegall Square North. Turn left up Donegall Place and eventually right into Donegall Street (avoiding Little Donegall Street on your left). Strike east towards Donegall Quay and then back towards Donegall Square, arriving at the junction of Donegall Square East with Donegall Square South. Continue in a southerly direction until you reach Donegall Pass, which turns into Donegall Road. This leads into Donegall Avenue, which is some way off from where you started.

Glossary

Ard — high
Soft — teeming down
Ard cheese — high cheddar
Crubeens — pig's trotters
Ballybunion — bad feet
Ballybogy — rotten cold
Curragh — boat or racecourse
Turlough — blind harpist
Esker — inquisitive Frenchman
Burren — Rock
Clint — different American film-star
Gryke — crack
Crack — talk
Torc — ring
Ring — Macgillycuddy's Reeks
Reek — Croagh
Croagh — Reek
Fleadh — féis
Sláinte — Up yours
Banshee — musical instrument
Tin whistle — unmusical instrument

Lambeg Drum — unwieldy instrument
Drum — hillock, ridge
Drumlin Belt — harness for percussion instruments
Fir — gents (or is it ladies?)
Mná — ditto
Muck — pig
Poke — ice-cream cornet
Muck muck — pig muck
Pig in a poke — there's something in my ice-cream
Pale — inferior English drink
Fadge — delectable sweet
Fudge — potato bread
Boxty — local dish made with potatoes
Champ — local dish made with potatoes
Boxing Champ — local boy made good on potatoes
Colcannon — local dish made with potatoes
Pratie — potato
Spud — potato
Potato — Murphy
Murphy — stout
Stout — Guinness or broad in the beamish
Guinness — plain
Plain — The Curragh
Dulse — edible seaweed
Yellow Man — inedible toffee
Yer Man — whatsisname

Further reading

Some useful publications —
Standing Stones of Ireland vols 1-27
Jaunting-Car Repairs Made Simple
More Standing Stones of Ireland
The Desmond O'Donnell Songbook From Old Photo-
    graphs
1001 Things to do with your Shamrock
Recumbent Standing Stones of Ireland: A Personal
    Selection
The Willie Yeats Bumper Fun Book (with pop-up
    characters)
Irish Shop Doorknobs